KU-213-419

WHY SHOULD I PROTECT NATURE?

Wayland

an imprint of Hodder Children's Books

WHY SHOULD I?

WHY SHOULD I Save Water?
WHY SHOULD I Save Energy?
WHY SHOULD I Protect Nature?
WHY SHOULD I Recycle?

Published in Great Britain in 2002 by Hodder Wayland,
an imprint of Hodder Children's Books
© Copyright 2002 Hodder Wayland

Commissioning editor: Vicky Brooker
Editor: Liz Gogerly
Designer: Jean Wheeler
Digital Colour: Carl Gordon

Produced in association with WWF-UK.
WWF-UK registered charity number 1081247.
A company limited by guarantee number
4016725. Panda device © 1986 WWF ®
WWF registered trademark owner.

British Library Cataloguing in Publication Data
Green, Jen, 1955–
Why should I Protect Nature?
1.Nature conservation – Juvenile literature
I.Title II.Gordon, Mike, 1948– III. Gogerly, Liz
IV. Protect nature
333.7'2

ISBN 07502 3682 5

Printed and bound in Italy by G. Canale &
C.Sp.A., Turin

Hodder Children's Books
A division of Hodder Headline Limited
338 Euston Road, London NW1 3BH

WHY SHOULD I PROTECT NATURE?

Written by Jen Green

Illustrated by Mike Gordon

HODDER
Wayland

an imprint of Hodder Children's Books

Nature is the big, wild world all around us, from giant oak trees to little acorns and wiggling worms.

The birds chirping
in the trees are part
of nature ...

so is the salty
smell of the sea ...

6

sploshing in rain
puddles ...

and the soft fur on
a donkey's nose ...

7

8

On our trip, we went to the sea and looked in rockpools. It was great!

On the way home,
we had a picnic
in a wood.

Everyone got a bit rowdy.
Craig and Marina broke
some branches,

I threw my
drinks can,

John picked
some flowers

and Sally
tried to swat
a bee.

Our teacher, Miss Wade, said we should protect nature, not hurt it.

14

She said, 'What do you think would happen if everyone broke off branches?'

'The trees would
have no leaves left,
and they couldn't
grow properly.
Birds couldn't nest in
their branches.

And guess what would happen if we all picked flowers and swatted bees?'

'There would be
no flowers left,

and we'd have
no honey for
breakfast.

18

'The countryside would be knee-deep in paper, plastic and tin cans.

Birds and animals could choke or get trapped in litter, and die.'

'Instead of picking flowers, we could sow wild flowers in a corner of the garden.

Butterflies and bees love flowers,
so they'll visit too.'

'We could plant a tree
instead of breaking
branches.

26

Clearing up litter keeps nature looking lovely, and helps animals and birds.'

27

Now we have fun
looking after nature.

After all,
people are
part of
nature too!

Notes for parents and teachers

Why Should I? **and the National Curriculum**

The *Why Should I?* series satisfies a number of requirements for the *Personal, Social and Health Education* framework at Key Stage 1. There are four titles about the environment in the series: *Why Should I ... Save Water? Save Energy? Recycle?* and *Protect Nature?* Within the category of *Citizenship*, these books will help young readers to think about simple environmental issues, and other social and moral dilemmas they may come across in everyday life. Within the category of *Geography*, the books will help children to understand environmental change and how to recognize it in their own surroundings, and also help them to discover how their environment may be improved and sustained. Within the category *Developing confidence and responsibility*, thinking about recycling will also teach children to consider others and to act unselfishly.

Why Should I Protect Nature? introduces the topic of the environment – the natural world around us, whether we live in a city or the country. It introduces the fact that humans can harm nature, but we can also help to protect it. The book introduces a number of simple tasks which children can carry out to help protect the natural world.

Suggestions for reading the book with children

As you read the book with children, you may find it helpful to stop and discuss issues as they come up in the text. Children might like to reread the story, taking on the role of different characters. Which character in the book reflects their own attitude to nature most closely? How do their opinions differ from those expressed in the book?

The book describes a number of ways in which people can harm nature, including dropping litter, picking flowers and harming animals and insects. Will anyone admit to doing any of these things? The book discusses the consequences of such actions, especially if everyone were to do the same. Introduce the idea that the natural world is also harmed by pollution caused by waste from farms and

30

factories but also from our homes and cities. Pollution may damage the air, water or the soil under our feet.

The end of the book introduces the idea that humans are also part of nature. Like all animals, we need clean air to breathe, water to drink, and space in which to live. Plants and animals provide us with all our food and help to make the world fit to live in. Discuss the idea that we cannot live without the natural world and stress that this is why it is vital that we learn to protect it – for our own as well as nature's sake.

Reading the book and discussing the protection of nature may introduce children to a number of unfamiliar words, including agriculture, environment, extinct, habitat, industry, litter, pollution, recycling. Make a list of all the new words and discuss what they mean.

Suggestions for follow-up activities

Children may have gone on an outing to the coast or countryside similar to the one described in the book. Encourage them to describe their own experiences and feelings using the book as a framework. They might like to write an account of their trip, or alternatively make up a story about an imaginary visit to the coast or countryside. The stories could be put together to make a class book.

The book introduces a number of simple ways in which we can help to protect nature, such as picking up litter and making a wild flower garden. Take a trip to the local park to study conditions there, and investigate how humans are helping and harming nature locally. Children might like to create a wild flower area in a corner of the playground or in the garden at home. Other ideas for helping to protect nature include organizing a local litter clean-up, and not using pesticides on the garden. Children might like to build a simple bird table or make a small pond for water creatures using an old washing-up bowl. Do the children have other ideas to help protect the natural world?

Books to read

Dear Greenpeace by Simon James (Walker Books, 1991)
When Emily discovers a whale living in her pond, she writes to Greenpeace, an organization which helps to protect nature. Many letters are exchanged, as Emily discovers more about her whale.

Grimbleton Zoo is Closing Down by Keith Brumpton
(Macdonald Young Books, 1995)
A long poem about the struggle to save a local zoo, illustrated with cartoons. When Grimbleton Zoo is forced to close because of lack of money, the people of the nearby town try to adopt the animals, with hilarious results.

How Green Are You? by David Bellamy (Frances Lincoln, 1998)
A cartoon book by a well-known nature expert, that explains all about the natural world and how we can help to protect it.

What do we think about Our Environment? by Malcolm Penny
(Hodder Wayland, 1999)
An information book that explains all about the natural world and how humans are harming it. Includes practical ideas for helping to protect nature.